From the Bible

Miracles
of Jesus

Retold and Illustrated

By

Chris Botha

Narrow Way Publishers

Miracles of Jesus

From the Bible

Miracles of Jesus

Unless otherwise indicated all scripture quotations are taken from the King James Version of the Bible.

Retold and Illustrated

by

Chris Botha

Narrow Way Publishers

Dedication

For Laura, Sarah and Matthew

Contents

Introduction

I have retold some of the miracles that are recorded in the gospels that Jesus performed. These are just a few and there are many more. The Bible informs us that if all the things that Jesus did were written down, all the books in the world would not be able to tell of them.

*And there are also many other things which Jesus did, the which, if they should be written every one, I suppose that even the world itself could not contain the books that should be written. Amen. **John 21:25***

Jesus did these things so that people would be able to know who he was, the very son of God and the saviour of the world.

As we look at Jesus, we see what God the Father is like, because Jesus said, "If you have seen me you have seen the Father". In Jesus we can see what the heavenly Father is like. When we see what motivated Jesus, we know what motivates the Father. God is love, and Jesus displayed that love nature of the Father for people. That is why he loved and still loves the people, teaches them and heals them.

I trust that by reading this you will be encouraged and understand more about Jesus and will grow an unconquerable faith in the Lord Jesus Christ. May you be inspired to discover in a very personal way this incomparable one who came out from the presence of the Father.

My prayer and intention with this work is that you will enjoy these wonderful miracles that Jesus did, know that he is still in the miracle business and learn to trust God.

For this purpose the Son of God was manifested, that he might destroy the works of the devil. **1 John 3:8**

Chris Botha

Miracle

The *Chambers 21ˢᵗ Century Dictionary* defines a miracle like this:

Miracle : "an act or event that breaks the laws of nature, and is therefore thought to be caused by the intervention of God or another supernatural force"

9

1.

The First Miracle

U p to the time of this story we are told that Jesus had done no miracles yet. He had grown up and lived in the small town of Nazareth and the people knew him simply as the carpenter's son.

A very unusual prophet had appeared in the country and he was preaching out in the wilderness of Judaea. His name was John and crowds of people from Jerusalem and across the country were going out to hear the message that he preached. He was baptizing people in the Jordan at a place called Betha Bara, which means "Ferry House".

John was not a slick or refined preacher and he was not dressed in the finest clothes. He shouted out his message to those who came to hear that they should repent of their sins and warned them of the coming judgement. He wore rough clothes made of camel skin. He lived off the land and he ate locusts and wild honey. When people repented of their sin John baptized them in the waters of the Jordan River.

Many people were waiting for God's messiah to come. When John the Baptist had seen Jesus coming to be baptized, he cried out loud to the people:

"This is the one that God has sent!"

The Spirit of God had told John that he would know who the Messiah was because the Holy Spirit of God would come upon him and would remain on him. When Jesus came up out of the water John saw the Holy

Spirit in the shape of a dove. The Holy Spirit came and stayed resting on Jesus. John declared that he heard a voice from heaven saying.

"This is my greatly loved son. Listen to him!" spoke out the voice of the Father, out of heaven.

John the Baptist had many disciples who followed him and believed that he had been sent by God. John stood with his disciples standing around him and watched Jesus as he was walking on his way.

"Look, here is the Lamb of God, who takes away the sins of the world!" he called out in a loud voice as he pointed to Jesus.

When his disciples heard John say this some of them left him and immediately began to follow Jesus.

"What are you looking for?" Jesus said to them when he saw they were following him.

"We want to know where you live," they replied to Jesus.

"Come and see," said Jesus.

So it was that there were those of John's followers who heard what John had to say and they began to follow Jesus. This did not upset John but rather he was happy about this. He knew that he was not the Messiah but that his job was to prepare the way for him and to point out that Jesus was the Messiah of God.

One of John's followers was a man called Andrew, and he was one of those who began to follow Jesus. He was very excited that he had found

God's Messiah and so he first went to find his brother Simon to tell him.

"Come!" Andrew said, "We have found the special one that God has sent!"

When Jesus saw Simon, he seemed to know him even though they had not yet met. Before Andrew could introduce Simon, Jesus said to him:

"Your name is Simon, which means you are like a blowing reed, but your name will be Peter because you will be stable like a rock."

So it was that the two brothers began to be Jesus' followers together. They stayed with Jesus that day.

The next day Jesus went and found a man called Philip, and he said to him, "Follow me!"

15

Philip in turn went and found a man called Nathanael.

"Come and see who I have found," said Philip. "This is God's special Person, the Messiah."

"Where is he from?" asked Nathanael.

"He is from Nazareth," said Philip.

What?" said Nathanael. "Can anything good come out of Nazareth?"

"Just come and see for yourself!" said Philip.

As they were coming Jesus looked up and saw them.

Before they could say anything, Jesus looked at Nathanael with great love, "Ah," he said. "You are a real Israelite."

"How do you know me," asked Nathanael, "because we have never met?"

"I saw you when you were sitting under the fig tree," said Jesus. "Before Philip called you."

Nathanael knew then that Jesus was a prophet because he could not know this unless the Spirit of God had revealed it to him. Only a true prophet could know and see things like this without even being there. He began to follow Jesus.

Now there was a wedding in the little town of Cana in the part of the country known as Galilee which was close by. Jesus was invited to the wedding and so were his followers and so they went.

Everyone was having a great time at the celebration of the wedding and they were all feasting and enjoying themselves. Jesus' mother was at the wedding too and she called him quietly to one side to talk to him.

"We have run out of wine," said his mother.

"It's not my time to speak yet," said Jesus.

Mary, Jesus' mother, called the servants and told them, "Do whatever he tells you to do."

At the wedding there were six big pots that were used for the guests to wash their hands.

Jesus pointed to them, and told the waiters, "Fill those pots up with water!"

When the waiters had done that Jesus said to them, "Now scoop out some of that and take it to the head table to be tasted."

The servants did just what Jesus had told them to. When the master of ceremonies at the wedding had tasted the water that was now wine and no longer water, he was astonished.

"This is the best wine we have had so far at the wedding," he said as he gave some to the others at the main table. "Why did you keep this for last? We should have had this wine first because it is so good."

This was the first miracle that we know Jesus did. There would be many more. His disciples were astonished at what Jesus had done. They would see Jesus do many more wonders and miracles as they followed him wherever he would take them.

2.

Jairus and the Touch

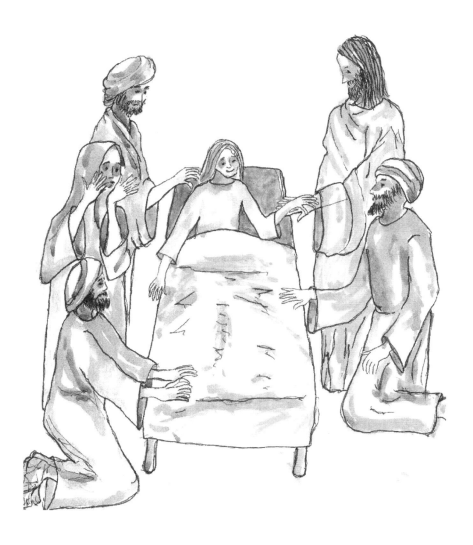

Jesus' kindliness and his loving smile draw the people to come to him and when they come, they are not disappointed. When the disciples want to keep the children away from Jesus because he is too busy, he tells them to let the little ones come and not to keep them away. The mothers and fathers watch as he takes the little ones in his arms and blesses them. He puts his hands on the children and speaks his blessing over them. The parents are touched and there are tears that they cannot hide as they see this love in action. It is so unlike the stiff, untouchable tradition of the scribes and pharisees.

The teacher takes time to teach the people who are desperate for the words of God. There has not been a true prophet in Israel for four hundred years. Now Jesus is sitting teaching a big group of people who have made themselves as comfortable as they can to hear his messages. As Jesus is speaking there is a disturbance in the listening crowd. Someone is pushing his way through the crowd that is carefully listening to Jesus.

The disruption is caused by a very well-dressed man, who is quite obviously well off and of some influence. Jesus stops speaking as the man makes his way with some difficulty through the people who sit and have been hanging on every word that Jesus speaks. Even though the man wears such beautiful clothes, he is unconcerned about his appearance because his mission is most important and urgent. After much effort and upsetting and unsettling many in the crowd who must move for him to get by, he eventually gets to Jesus.

The disciples are about to prevent the man from getting any closer, but Jesus silently raises a hand for them to not do that. In obvious distress the man falls to the ground out of breath and panting hard. The ground is dusty, and it sticks to his beautiful clothes, but he does not seem to be concerned about that. When he lifts his pleading face to Jesus it is tear-stained, and the tears mix with the brown of the fine dust on his cheeks. There is something more important to him than his expensive clothes or his dignity.

Jesus looks at him in that familiar way that he has as though he is the only one there. Even though they are surrounded by this big crowd, to the man they all disappear, and he sees only Jesus. Jesus waits for the panting man to speak but for a few moments the man is out of breath because he has come as fast as he can. He is not used to running any more. The people have grown silent. They know what great need fells like, what it looks like. They understand because they well recognize desperation when they see it. Some of the people present know the man well because he is the leader of the local synagogue, in the nearby little town. His town is not so very far away, and he is highly respected and loved by his friends and neighbours. Many of the onlookers know of his care for all those in his community.

The man's name is Jairus, and he is still breathless so that Jesus waits for him to regain his breath until he is able to speak. He manages to get his first words out.

"Lord," Jairus says to Jesus, looking up as he kneels on the dusty soil, "My daughter may even now be already dead. But I know that if you come and put your hands on her that she will live."

Jairus has tears running down his cheeks as his one thought is of his beautiful, young daughter. She is such a joy to him, and he loves her so much. Some in the listening crowd make sounds of sympathy as they hear of the little girl and of the sad plight that Jairus is in.

Jesus looks at Jairus and loves him very much.

"I will come," says Jesus, and immediately gets up to go with this desperate father: all else set aside.

The crowd make way for Jesus and the man Jairus, to pick their way, to Jairus's house. Jesus starts off down the road with Jairus at his side. He is closely followed by his protective disciples who are trying to protect their master from the pushing crowd. The people who have been sitting listening to him do not want to be left behind. They really do want to see what is going to happen and what Jesus will do.

So it is that a big crowd moves along, with some running to keep up with Jesus and his disciples. There are all kinds of people in the crowd. Many are poor, many are sick, but they are still able to keep up. They bump into and jostle each other, and all want to see what Jesus is going to do now. The people love seeing the amazing things that he does because they are things that have never been seen before. They are amazed at how much time he spends with them and how much he loves them. They feel that they have been neglected for so long and that is why they try their best to stay as close as they can. You don't see these things every day.

The dust of the well-trodden road rises in the air stirred up by the sandaled feet of the throng as it scuffs, shuffles and strides over the chalky surface. There are those further back in the crowd who cough and cover their mouths and noses. They need some rain to have less dust but then they think it will just turn muddy.

Unnoticed in the crowd there is a woman who is also trying her best to keep up and to get as close to Jesus as she can. She has a very good reason for trying to get to Jesus. Nobody else knows that what she is doing is not only wrong. What she is doing is illegal. But she is a desperate woman. She will have to keep her secret and so she pulls her veil over her face. Her face is determined but thin and pale and her eyes are dull and sunken from her years of illness. She is not used to the bright sunlight and maybe she should have just stayed at home.

What is not a secret is all the news that is being spoken about Jesus and all that he is doing. This news is spreading like wildfire through the towns and villages. It is because of this news that has reached this thin, little woman that she is here, out in public and jostling along in this moving crowd. This is taking all her effort and strength just to come so far, and she is determined, and it is that determination that is what shows most on her drawn face.

Like many others this woman has heard about all the wonders and miracles that Jesus is performing. There are so many that Jesus has healed from terrible sicknesses and diseases. He just speaks to some and they are healed. He touches other sick people, and they are healed because of his touch. Then there are still others who are just put down along the roadsides. All that they do is to reach out and touch Jesus' clothes as he walks past. When they touch only his clothes they are immediately healed.

This woman has a sickness that means that no-one is permitted to touch her. She is not allowed out in public. No-one in the crowd knows that or she would be in serious trouble. She is bumping and touching people all around her as they all walk along. She must get close to Jesus. If she is found out she could be put to death.

This woman has been suffering for twelve long years. She has been to so many doctors. She has suffered through so many different remedies and medicines that don't work. She has spent everything that she has. Nothing has helped and nothing has made her in the least bit better. The things that the doctors have tried have rather made everything worse.

She remembers the things that her neighbours told her about Jesus.

When she hears about the things that he is doing she begins to hope again that maybe she can get better. That day she makes up her mind because she hears that Jesus is just down the road from her house. Is this her chance? She cries as she stands in her dark house. She thinks about how sick she has been and still is. How long has it been? She can hardly remember what it feels like to be well and she wipes the tears from her eyes at the thought. She must get going and not let this opportunity pass.

"I will just touch the hem of his clothes," she repeats to herself as she goes along, "I will be made completely well."

She keeps muttering this to herself. Now here she is. The people jostle and push her. She feels weak.

She pushes on. Almost there. She makes a big effort to get close to Jesus and in an unexpected moment she is right there. Jesus is there walking just in front of her. No-one will notice, she thinks as she reaches out her hand and touches the edge of Jesus' clothes. As her fingers touch, there is something that comes out of Jesus and goes into her body and she feels everything change. Afterwards she will find it difficult to describe to others that it felt like a jolt from Jesus into her body. It is only because of the crowd pushing in on all sides that she manages to keep standing. The feeling of weakness is gone, and she no longer has that sick feeling that she has had for so many years. Now it is gone.

That very moment Jesus stops, and the crowd stops as well. Everyone wonders what is going on as Jesus turns around so that for the first time the woman comes face-to-face with him. The crowd grows quiet. Some in the back who can't see are grumbling and wondering what is happening now.

"Who touched me?" says Jesus.

"What do you mean Master?" ask his disciples. "Everyone is touching you in this crowd."

"No. Someone deliberately touched me," insists Jesus, "because I felt power leaving me."

The woman bows down at Jesus' feet because she can't help it. What will happen now that she has been found out? The woman admits that she is the one who has touched him and trembling still from the healing power that has gone into her she tells him her story. He looks at her as though he already knows it.

"Take courage daughter," says Jesus, smiling at her. "Your faith makes you completely well."

Jesus is still speaking to the woman who has now been healed when an out of breath messenger arrives. He comes from Jairus's house and his expression shows how upset he is because he has bad news.

"Don't worry the teacher any longer," is the messenger's blunt news to Jairus. "Your daughter is already dead."

When Jesus hears the words of the messenger, he looks at Jairus but Jairus says nothing. He only looks into the face of Jesus.

"Don't be afraid. Only believe and she will be completely well," said Jesus with calm assurance.

Jesus walks on with Jairus and the crowd begins to move again and soon they arrive at Jairus's house. The relatives and friends have heard the tragic news and they have all gathered at the house and they are already crying and wailing. They say the little girl is dead.

"Do not cry like that," Jesus tells the people. "The child is not dead. She is only sleeping."

When the many mourners hear these words, they begin to laugh and mock Jesus and what he has said. Jesus only allows Peter, James and John and the mother and father of the girl into the house.

Inside, the little group stands with Jesus in the little girl's bedroom. She lies quiet and still on her bed. Jesus takes the little girl by the hand and says to her, "Little girl, get up!"

When he says those words the little girl's spirit comes back into her and she sits up, on the bed. There is a gasp of joy around the room at this and great relief and laughter as the parents hug and hold their little girl.

"You need to give her something to eat," Jesus says matter-of-factly to her Mum and Dad. "Don't tell anyone what just happened here."

3.

A Broken Roof

Jesus loves the little city of Capernaum. He has a house there which he uses as his base. Capernaum is a pleasant seaside town on the shores of the Sea of Galilee. Jesus is in the house this day. The news spreads quickly through the whole town. People quickly come from everywhere and a huge crowd gathers. This is a normal thing. Soon the house is full and surrounded by people. The crowd is so big that no-one else can get in or out of the house. There are people at the door. They are gathered at the windows. All want to hear and see what Jesus is saying and doing.

Everyone has been told of the wonderful things that the teacher does. They have heard about the many people that have been healed and the amazing miracles that Jesus performs. There is great faith throughout the town.

Jesus sits in the house and teaches the people. He speaks about the kingdom of God. Outside, the crowd continue to gather. There is no more standing room. There are curious faces at the windows. The door is jammed with desperate shapes. They press up against each other.

There is even more commotion outside. A group of men try to get to the door of the house. The people don't move. They have come to hear Jesus themselves and they are not going to give way.

"You'll not get in there," some say. "You've got no chance!"

They are right. There is no way. The group cannot get through. There are four men. They are quite young. They have a fifth man that they are carrying on a stretcher. He is their friend. They have brought him so that Jesus will heal him. The poor man lying on the stretcher cannot walk at all. He can't use his arms either.

The four have brought their sick friend a long way. They are not about to give up this easily. They go aside from the crowd. They begin to discuss what they will do. They decide that if they can't get in through the door or a window there is only one other way. That way is the roof.

The roof of the house is flat like all the houses in the town. There is a step up there on the other side. There are no windows on that side of the house and no other people. With some huffing and puffing they manage to get their friend up onto the flat roof. He is still on the stretcher, trusting that his friends won't drop him.

"Well we're up here now," puffs one of the friends.

"Now what?" says a second.

"We have to go through and down," says the boldest man who had the idea in the first place.

"Who's going to pay for the damage?" says the fourth and they all shrug.

The four look at each other. They will sort that out later. They know all too well what they will now have to do. They start.

"Let's try to be careful," says the most considerate man.

"Yeah, sure," says one of the friends, breaking off the first tiles.

They all begin to break away at the roof. At first, they only have a small hole. They keep going until they have a bigger hole. They can see through and down into the room where Jesus is. They can hear Jesus' voice now as he is teaching the people. Jesus just continues to speak as though what they are doing does not worry him. The four friends keep going to make the hole in the roof big enough for their helpless friend on the stretcher to fit through. They realize that Jesus has stopped talking. Their four faces peer down through the now big hole they have made. In the house the surprised faces look back up at them.

The four men tie rope that they have to the four corners of the stretcher. They have come this far. No point stopping now. They let their friend down, right in front of where Jesus sits. Jesus is quite calm as he watches. He smiles. He looks up at the hole in the roof where the faces of the four friends peer down through the hole at him. He looks pleased. His eyes light up. He recognises the faith that they have.

Jesus looks at the man on the stretcher who is now right there in front of him. He loves helping these people.

"Son," Jesus says to the man. "Your sins are forgiven."

Jesus looks around. Sitting right there are some of the cleverest men in the country. He watches the frowns on their faces. He knows what they are thinking without them saying a word. They are thinking that Jesus is saying something wrong. They are very religious.

"How can a man forgive someone's sins?" they think. "Only God can forgive sins!"

"Why are you thinking these things?" asks Jesus. "What is easier to say? 'Your sins are forgiven.' Or 'Take up your bed and walk.' You need to know that I have the power to forgive sins on earth."

Jesus turns to the man still lying on his stretcher.

"Get up!" Jesus commands the man. "Pick up your bed and go home!"

As soon as Jesus says that, the man immediately gets up. It is something he could not do before. His eyes grow wide as he realizes what he has just done. He is standing. He picks up the stretcher on which he has been lying. He realizes then that his arms are working. He pushes his way through the crowd of amazed people. He feels as though he is in a daze. It feels wonderful. The people are so quiet and move aside as he comes. The healed man walks as though in a dream. His heart is skipping with joy.

The four friends on the roof can't help it. They shout and clap. The crowd all seem to shout out at once. They have never seen anything like this before in their lives.

Jesus is smiling. He stands and so do his disciples. As the crowd begins to clear the way he leads them out of the house. The disciples look at each other in astonishment. The sea breeze blows fresh faith against their faces. They look at this one that they follow. He walks just a pace ahead of them. Their hearts are full. Full of the things that they have seen. Full of the things they have heard. Their thoughts are racing. Their thinking of what is possible is changing. What else will they see?

4.

The Pool of Bethesda

There is great excitement. The crowds of people are cheerful as they are go up to the feast. People meet old friends. There is the sound of happy children in the streets. There is going to be a special festival for the Jewish people. Jesus also is on his way to Jerusalem to celebrate it. On his way into the city he passes the place where the sheep gate is. The sheep gate is close to the wall of the city and near the entrance to the temple. This is where those who come to worship at the temple buy sheep for sacrifices. There is the sound of the bleating of sheep and the lowing of cattle. The familiar smell of sheep and cows hangs in the air.

On his way to the temple Jesus needs to pass a place that is well known to the people. It is a popular spot. It is like a swimming pool but a very special one. The people here are not just there to swim or just relax. Oh no! Around this pool there are lying a big crowd of desperate people. Some of these people are blind. Some are lame and can't walk. Some have arms or legs that don't work right.

It is quiet beside the pool. Not much seems to be happening. There is a good reason that all these sick people to come to this place. This is called the Pool of Bethesda. Bethesda means "house of mercy", and those who come here certainly need mercy. Many friends or relatives of these unfortunate ones drop them off at the pool in the morning. They then go about their day and collect them again in the evening to take them home again.

It would be strange if you didn't know the detail about this place and you just see these very sick, helpless people all waiting. You would wonder what they could possibly be waiting for. They all want to get better. To be healed. There is always something quite strange and unusual that will happen from time to time at this pool. Nobody knows when. They all know that every now and then a quite amazing thing will happen. An angel will come down without any warning. The angel will stir the water of the pool. You can tell. One moment the pool is quite still, but when the angel comes you know. The water begins to move and make ripples and lots of swirling circles spread across the pool. This is what everyone is waiting for. When the angel comes the water gets churned up. The first ones who get into the water after that will be immediately healed. It doesn't matter what the sickness is. Whatever problem the person has immediately disappears. Some say that they know of some who have seen the angel. One thing is sure, that even if you can't see the angel you can see the water all swirling and stirred up when he does come.

Jesus stops at the pool. He doesn't seem to be in a hurry. The disciples know he is always being led by the Holy Spirit of God and that means that there will be something that Jesus will now do. Jesus goes in and his disciples go with him.

The pool has five porches under which most of the sick lie. It shelters them from the hot sun or the rain. The beautiful curves of the round arches stretch high around the pool. Jesus stands a moment and sees these who have come for mercy. He takes in the sight of all the people waiting and hoping to be made well. The disciples see that Jesus' attention is drawn to a man lying close by them. He is paralyzed and so cannot walk at all. The man lies on a mat in the shade of the porch. Jesus begins to talk to the man.

"How long have you been like this?" Jesus asks the man.

"I've been like this for thirty-eight years," says the man.

"Would you like to get well?" asks Jesus.

"I do want to get well," says the man, "but every time the angel stirs up the water, before I can get into the water it is too late. Others always get in before me."

"Well stand up," Jesus says to the man. "Pick up your mat and go home."

Jesus' words have a remarkable effect on the man. He immediately gets up, which he could never do before. He picks up the mat he has been lying on as Jesus has told him to. The man walks off to go home testing his legs that he has never been able to use before. The place is very crowded. Many are helping their sick friends or family. Jesus makes his way off into and through the crowd. They continue their journey up to the temple.

Now this is the Sabbath day for the Jewish people. That means that they are supposed to rest. They are not supposed to walk more than a certain distance. They are certainly forbidden to do any kind of work. The healed man carrying his bed is going home just like Jesus told him. He walks past the temple and some Jewish leaders stop him. They are outraged that he is carrying his bed on the Sabbath day. Strictly this is not allowed.

"You can't carry your bed on the Sabbath day," they say to the man. "You are not supposed to. It's against the law."

"The man who healed me told me to pick up my bed and go home," explains the man.

"Who is this man who healed you?" ask the Jewish leaders.

"I'm not sure who he is," says the man. "There are such big crowds.

So many people. I don't know who he is."

The man who is now healed doesn't want to get into any trouble. He immediately drops the mat he is carrying right there on the roadside. He decides to go up to the temple. He has a lot to be thankful to God for. He hasn't been able to go to the temple for thirty-eight years. He sees Jesus there in the temple as well. He is so glad to see him

Jesus stands in the temple with his disciples. He is at home in his Father's house. He recognizes the man he has healed when he comes in. The man is overjoyed to see Jesus again. Jesus puts his hand on his shoulder. He speaks kindly to him. He is so pleased to see the man well, rejoicing and in the temple.

"Now that you are healed and well, don't do unbelieving things any longer," says Jesus. "You don't want to get sick again or have something even worse happen."

The man is so happy and proud of Jesus. He goes to tell the Jewish leaders who asked him that it is Jesus who has healed him.

"There is the man who healed me," says the man pointing to Jesus who is now talking to some other people. "He made me completely well, as you can see."

The religious leaders in the temple are outraged that Jesus has healed the lame man on the sabbath day.

"Did you heal this man on the sabbath day?" they ask Jesus in threatening voices.

"My Father is always working, and I also am working!" Jesus replies undeterred by their threats.

What Jesus says in answer to their threats and their threatening behaviour makes them even more angry and murder rises in their hearts. They want to kill this one who threatens their powerless religion. They understand all too well the meaning of Jesus' words. By calling God his Father he is making himself equal with God.

The people in the temple know that this remarkable miracle has taken place to this man who was born lame and so has been lame for all of his thirty-eight years of life. Many of them know the man well and the miracle cannot be discounted or discredited. The religious leaders can do nothing against Jesus now because the people will stone them because they regard Jesus as a true and great prophet. The religious leaders decide to wait for their chance. With evil in their hearts they make up their minds that they will eventually have their opportunity to trap this one who is such a threat to them.

5.

Jesus Feeds the People

T he evil king Herod had thrown John into prison and then had done an even more evil thing because he had John beheaded. Herod was a very superstitious man and fearful of things he did not understand. When he heard about Jesus and the miraculous things that he was doing he did not understand this. Those closest to him who were also very superstitious as well did not know either. Some said that this was John Baptist risen from the dead, and that thought sent shivers of fear through Herod. Others said that it was Elijah who had come back again. Still others said that it was one of the old prophets come back again, and that was why he was able to do such wonders and miracles.

Jesus had sent his twelves disciples that he called apostles, or ones who are sent, into all the towns and villages in the area. He gave them authority over all demons and power to heal all kinds of diseases. When they came back to Jesus, they were amazed at what they had been able to do. Jesus took them aside into a quiet place to spend time with them. They went to a place out in the countryside near the town of Bethsaida, which was where Peter, Andrew and Philip came from. When the people heard that Jesus was there, they went out in their hundreds and thousands to him there.

These many hundreds and even thousands of people who went to hear Jesus teach were now far away from their homes or towns or villages. Many were there, desperate to be healed. There were many with horrible sicknesses and diseases. So many people. There was not enough room for them in the cities or towns. Jesus began now to have these crowds come to him outside of the towns and cities. He chose places way out in the countryside.

The news that he was there would quickly spread. The people would quickly find out that he was there. As soon as they knew where he was, they would come to him from all around. He would take time to teach them about God's Kingdom. Out in the desert places there would be more room. There would be the space for the thousands of people who came to Jesus.

At the time of this story a wicked and evil thing had happened. John the

Baptist was baptizing people in the Jordan River. John had told the people publicly that King Herod had done evil. It was reported to King Herod about what John had been saying about him. Herod who was a quick-tempered and angry man had John arrested and thrown into prison. The king then did something even worse. He had John the Baptist killed.

John's disciples came and told Jesus what had happened. When Jesus heard this horrible news, he took to a ship with his disciples and headed for the other side of the Sea of Galilee. It was a desert place. It would be quiet there. The news of where Jesus was could not be hidden and so the crowds heard where Jesus had gone, and they also began to follow.

Way out in a dry part of the countryside the large crowds of thousands flocked to Jesus. He taught them many things about the kingdom of God. It was getting late in the afternoon and Jesus had finished his teaching. He took a drink from a water bottle and the crowds sat back too. The people were content and deeply encouraged at the things that Jesus spoke. Many had been healed and had no more pain in their bodies. They felt that God was hearing their cries for help, and that help had arrived for them. Jesus sat back for a moment to catch his breath. His disciples sat around him. Jesus spoke to his disciples. They were the chosen ones who had answered his call of "Follow me!". They sat closest to him.

"The people have been out here with us for three days," said Jesus.

The twelve heard him and nodded. They too had endured for that time, out in the countryside.

"Why don't we send them away so that they can get food from the villages," suggested the disciples who had been thinking about the situation that they found themselves in.

"I don't want to send them away hungry," said Jesus, "because they may be too weak to make the journey home. They haven't eaten in all the time they have been with us. I don't want to send them away like that."

The disciples looked at each other, helplessly. What could they possibly do about the people's need for food? Between them all they didn't have any good ideas.

"How are we going to give so many people something to eat?" said one of them.

"We are here way out in the wilderness," said another.

"There is nowhere to get food out here," said a third.

"How many loaves of bread do you have?" asked Jesus.

The disciples all looked at what they had brought and counted the number of loaves that they had between them.

"We have five loaves," said one.

"And two fishes," said another, wondering with a smile what difference that could possibly make.

Jesus stood and lifted his hands to show the crowd that he wanted to speak. The people stopped what they were doing. They grew quiet, waiting for what this wonderful teacher would say. They loved the words that he spoke to them. They listened to him carefully. They waited to hear what he would say now. What would he do? Most of them were standing to stretch their legs.

"I want you all to sit down, on the ground," he said. "Find a good place on the grass, and everyone sit down,".

Jesus' voice carried out across the crowd. The people began to sit down. They had no idea what he was about to do, but they trusted him. They found places where the new green grass had grown through from the recent rains. They chose places of soft tufts of grass.

"Bring the loaves of bread and fish to me," said Jesus to his disciples.

They brought Jesus the five loaves of bread and the two fish in a basket. He told his disciples they each needed a basket and so they each brought an empty basket to him. Jesus took the bread and lifted it up to heaven. He spoke a blessing over the food. Then he began to break the loaves and the fish into pieces. As he broke the bread and the fish, he gave the pieces to his disciples in their baskets. As each disciple's basket filled up, they in turn gave the pieces of bread and fish to the people. The crowds sat now on the ground. The disciples kept doing that going back and forth between Jesus and the groups of people. They kept going back and forth to Jesus and then to the people. Jesus kept breaking the bread and the fish into pieces. Before they knew it, they had given food to all the thousands of people.

The people were eating. They were no longer hungry. They were full. They sat back on the green grass satisfied. The people had no idea where the food was coming from. Only the disciples knew about the miracle that was happening.

"Collect up all the food that hasn't been eaten, because we don't want to waste anything. See how much food there is left over," said Jesus.

The disciples went around the groups of people. They collected up twelve baskets of food that were left over. There were at least five thousand men there as well as women and children.

The disciples looked at each other. Had that really happened? They were amazed. They were always amazed at what Jesus did. They had seen another miracle. Right before their own eyes. They looked at their hands that had handed out so much food, then they looked at Jesus, their miracle worker. They realized then that they themselves had not eaten. Jesus looked at his twelve disciples.

"Help yourself," said Jesus with a smile.

He pointed at the twelve baskets that the twelve apostles held. Each one held a basket filled with good food.

They knew that he would never forget them.

6.

The Storm and Gadara

J esus had finished his teaching and he sent the people away to go to their homes. The evening was closing in. Jesus and his disciples were left on the shore.

"Let's go to the other side of the lake," Jesus said to them,

There was no time to eat or clean themselves up. Jesus went just as he was. They set off across the lake and other little boats were going along with them. They had been with crowds of people all day and Jesus was tired from a full day of teaching and praying for many of people.

The disciples could see that Jesus was weary from the day's work. He went to the back of the boat where he would be out of the way and where there was a cushion that they had prepared for him there. He lay down and was so tired from all he had done that day that he immediately fell fast asleep.

They started the journey well as the weather was fine and the sailing calm and pleasant. All seemed to be going well but unexpected storms do come down on the Sea of Galilee quite suddenly and this would be one of those times.

The storm that came was an unusually strong and violent one, even in the experience of the fishermen, who were used to these things. The wind began to blow a gale and the waves rose ever higher and became huge and threatening to their small fishing boat. The water crashed over the sides of the boat and dark clouds covered the sun. What had begun as a pleasant journey had now become a very dangerous journey. There was no turning back now because they were in the middle of the sea and were just as far from the land whether they went on or turned back.

The huge waves crashed and foamed over the open boat and it began to fill with water and began to sink lower in the water. The disciples did what they could and used whatever they could to bail out the water. They tried desperately to keep the boat afloat but the more water they bailed out the more water washed and crashed in. They felt they were losing the battle as the sea kept trying to fill the boat.

The noise of the storm was deafening with the howling wind and the noisy crashing of huge waves. The rain that was torrenting down made things worse, as the thunder boomed across the heavens and lightning flashed menacingly above them. Their terrified shouting to each other could barely be heard above the storm's angry outburst. Everyone kept trying until finally it seemed to them to now be hopeless to stop the boat from sinking. Jesus was sleeping through it all.

The disciples had decided that they had lost their battle to keep afloat. Now they feared that all their lives would all be lost. Their hearts were filled with the fear that they would all drown, and it was in this state of great fright that they woke Jesus up. Surely, he would help them. Had he not instructed them to go to the other side of the sea.

"Teacher," they said, waking Jesus, "Don't you care whether we die or not?"

Jesus came as quickly awake as he had quickly fallen asleep. He said nothing in response to these words of his disciples. He stood in the boat that was pitching and rolling and as he held on to the mast he looked out over the storm and the waves. The wind blew the water into their faces. There was no fear in Jesus as he stood there in that small boat with a storm raging all around. There was a calm faith in his expression and the way he stood there that no storm could touch or trouble. With his free hand he pointed and spoke the words that would change everything.

"Peace!" he said. "Be still."

The words that Jesus spoke cut through the air and the tumult and there was an immediate change. With the warning in Jesus words the wind instantly stopped its fierce blowing and the sea, which rose in huge waves crashing over the boat, suddenly became quite flat and smooth like a barking, angry dog at the command of its master. The storm stopped. The boat sat now still on the quiet waters of the sea. The disciples' eyes widened as they looked at Jesus and then around at the quiet sea.

"Why are you so afraid?" said Jesus. "How is it that you have no faith?"

Those in the boat with Jesus were stunned and speechless by what Jesus had just done. How had this happened? How had Jesus by his words stopped the storm?

"What kind of man is this," they whispered to one another because they did not want Jesus to hear, "that even the wind and the sea obey him?"

They arrived on the other side of the lake and they landed in the country that belonged to the city of Gadara. This is where Jesus had planned to visit. Gadara was an important city in those days. It was one of a group of cities in that part of the country called the Decapolis, which means ten cities.

As the boat slid onto the shore the disciples looked up at the slopes that swept up from the shore into the steep hills. They pulled the boat up onto the beach and stretched from the hard work and being cramped up in the boat for so long. As they looked up the slopes, they could see many tombs covering the hillsides. This place gave the disciples the creeps. Many of the tombs had been carved out of the rocks. They were beautifully decorated in the Greek style. This place was well known in the area because there were many people living in the tombs.

When the boat was brought to the shore Jesus was the first to step on the land. No sooner had they arrived when they heard someone shrieking and shouting. They looked up and saw a man, dirty and naked and he was running down the hillside towards them. He did not look as though he wanted to make friends with these visitors landed from the sea. He shouted threats as he came, threw stones and cut himself as he came. The disciples had a pretty good idea that this was not looking good at all. They were thinking that this whole trip had been a big mistake. First the storm, and now this crazy person hurtling towards them.

The man looked a terrible mess, caked in dirt and with blood running down where he had wounded himself. The disciples braced themselves because it was obvious that this man was quite insane. He had lived for many years on the hillsides and in the tombs and caves themselves. A dirty demon had got a hold of him. He ran wild around the graves and would shout at anyone who would come near. He cut himself with stones. The people in the towns decided that he was dangerous. They didn't want him anywhere near them. Better if he stayed out there by the graves. A few times the people from the town had formed a posse to catch him and try to tame him but they couldn't manage it. At these times they had tied him with chains and ropes but each time he had snapped the ropes and chains and escaped. The demons that caused his madness made him very strong.

When the madman had seen the boat land, he had started running towards them, wildly down the steep slope to them. When Jesus had first seen the man, he understood immediately what the trouble was, and so he called out in a voice that felt like steel cutting through the air like a sword. The disciples had heard that authority in Jesus voice many times before.

"Come out of him you filthy demon!" Jesus had said to the demon that had captured this man while the man was still coming down the hill.

When the naked, dirty man got to where Jesus was on the beach he fell at Jesus' feet.

"What have I got to do with you, Jesus, you son of the highest God?" came a rasping voice from the man as he recognized who Jesus was and was terrified. "I beg you not to torment me."

"What is your name?" Jesus demanded of the demon.

"We are called Legion," rasped the voice from the man's throat, "because there are many of us."

The many demons who were tormenting the man began to beg Jesus not to send them out of the country or into the bottomless pit. They whined and whimpered. It happened that on a nearby hillside there was a big herd of pigs that was grazing. There were men from the town who were herding the pigs. The demons begged Jesus to let them go into the pigs.

"Go!" commanded Jesus and again his words cut through the air like a sharp sword.

Immediately the demons, terrified of Jesus, came out of the man and he flopped onto the ground. The pigs in the distance started acting crazy, squealing and running around madly. The men who were looking after them could not control them although they did try. The pigs squealing and jumping crazily ran headlong down the steep slope, not

Miracles of Jesus

stopping but running straight into the sea. The whole herd of pigs thrashed about in the deep waters of the sea and were all drowned right in front of them. The men who had been looking after them and had tried their best to stop the pigs saw that it was all over and they ran for their lives. They ran as fast as they could into the town to tell about what they had seen and what had happened to the pigs.

The pig herdsmen reported all about what had happened to the pigs and about the people who had come in the boat, and the man who had done this. A crowd gathered what with all the commotion that was being caused by the herdsmen. The owners didn't believe it at first because there were two thousand pigs in the herd, the whole town's pigs. How could they all possibly drown like that at the same time. There was a man down there who had done this the herders claimed. People from the town and the countryside who had been drawn together by all the noise and confusion decided that they wanted to see for themselves what had happened.

When the rabble from the town arrived, Jesus was still there with his disciples, on the shore. The people from the town were in a foul mood and were shouting and waving their arms angrily as they hurried along. How had they lost all their pigs? As they came up to Jesus and his disciples, they were met with an astonishing sight which caught them completely off guard. The crowd, now an angry mob, did not at first even recognise the man who had been mad and that was now free even though they knew him well. They had always been afraid of him but now there was the man and he was sitting listening quietly to Jesus. He did look a little like the same man when they looked more closely. Could this really be the same man?

"That's him!" said one of the herdsmen, pointing, not at the man, but at Jesus, the one who had done all this.

The man sat quite still. Sitting there, now fully clothed and in his right mind he looked quite normal. He did not look like his old self at all. He had washed himself and been given some fresh clothes and he listened to Jesus with the most wonderful look of peace and tranquillity on his face. The mob from the town were astonished but they were also very angry. They were not in the mood to be pleased that now the man was well. Rather they were very angry about the pigs. They would rather have the pigs back than the man.

When the crowd from the city looked at Jesus, they drew back as if in fright or dread and they all moved back in a wave some few paces. The sight of him and his very presence there in their country made them very afraid. The herders jabbered again at the pig owners about the pigs running into the sea.

Jesus being there deeply disturbed the townsfolk. They began to beg Jesus to leave their country because Jesus had made something change and they didn't like it at all. Things were not the way they liked them and the way they had been comfortable with before.

The man who was now free of that filthy demon and all the others as well that had tormented him, now sat quiet. He had a peace that he had not felt since he was a small child, and something had happened to him to start that horrible life of torment for so many years. The disciples began to prepare the boat because they could plainly see the ugly mood of the crowd. They wanted to leave, as soon as they possibly could. They had been right that this place was creepy what with the madness and the pigs and the many demons. The free man looked up at Jesus and he didn't want Jesus to leave at all and he was the only one from the city that felt that way. He began to plead with Jesus.

"Let me come with you, master," said the man, his eyes now shining clear and bright.

He wanted so much to go with this wonderful man. This man that had made him free again when no-one else could do anything for him.

"I want you to go back to your friends," said Jesus smiling at the man, to show that this was not a rejection. "Tell them how wonderful God has been to you."

The man knew how important Jesus' words were. As he walked away, again his own normal, healthy self, he decided that he would do just as Jesus said. He knew that he would be faithful to carry the message of Jesus, always. He would be forever grateful. He paused for a moment and turned, and he watched as Jesus and his disciples prepared to leave. They got into their boat and he waved as they pushed off from the shore. Jesus waved back and smiled and that would be the sight, the sight of Jesus' face, that would stay with him always.

As he walked back up the slope down which earlier, he had run controlled by the demons he breathed the fresh air coming from the sea and realized that he had found a new life. Jesus had done that for him, and because of that he devoted his life to travelling around that whole area, telling about Jesus, in all the ten cities in his country. He told the story everywhere and to everyone he came across about Jesus and what God had done for him. Everywhere he went the crowds gathered and listened to him.

They were amazed by what he told them. Some had known the man before and they were amazed by how his whole life had been forever changed.

7.

Jesus Catches Fish

J esus begins to travel from town to town in Galilee. When the people beg him to settle in their town, he tells them that he must go to the other towns as well, because that was why he has come. He preaches in the synagogues of the towns he comes to because his custom is to go to the synagogue on the Sabbath. He heals people of many different sicknesses and diseases. Jesus' fame is spreading far and wide. People hear about him as far away as Syria. They come from Judaea and around Jerusalem, and Samaria and then all of Galilee, where Jesus spends most of his time. When they discover where he is the crowds follow him as he travels around. They are eager to hear the things he teaches and to see the wonderful things that he does.

This day Jesus is walking by the sea and a big crowd has gathered to hear him. There are so many people on the beach that there is little room for Jesus. Jesus looks around for a solution and notices that there are two fishing boats there, pulled up on the shore. The fishermen have come in from a night of fishing out at sea. They have caught nothing. They are tired and disappointed. They are on the beach with their fishing things. They are cleaning and washing their nets getting ready to have another go a little later. Jesus smiles to himself as a heavenly idea occurs to him.

"Would you mind if I use your boat?" he says to one of the fishermen, whose name was Simon.

"That would be fine teacher," says Simon, who is a gruff man.

So it is that Jesus gets into Simon's boat. At Jesus request Simon pushes the boat out a little from the land and Jesus sits down in it. That is a sign to the people that he is about to teach the people. He begins to speak. The people on the shore move around into the bay and take up good places, some on rocks, or on the pebbly beach, some on the sand to listen. They can all see Jesus now and the sound of his voice reaches them clearly over the water, as it laps softly onto the shore.

The fishermen are still busy cleaning their nets, but they are still able to hear what Jesus is teaching. He talks about God's kingdom. They have heard tell about this teacher and now, here he is. Now they are listening to him for themselves and they feel a hope rise in them as his words begin to touch them. Maybe it won't be such a bad day after all.

There is something about the way this man is and what he says. Their hearts are moved in a way they have not experienced before. They pause in their work and sit still for a while, listening and watching this man sitting in the boat. Jesus continues to talk. His words seem to move something in them. They have not heard such clear understanding and wisdom before. After a while the fishermen's hands are still, the tasks forgotten and they simply sit listening. They have forgotten about the nets. The fish that they have not caught do not seem important now.

Jesus has finished speaking. He sits quietly and his words seem to wash quietly over the whole scene.

Then he speaks to Simon what Simon will forever after remember as though it were engraved on his heart.

"Push out a little from the shore," says Jesus, "and let down your nets for a catch."

"Master," Simon says, and then begins to explain, "We have worked hard all night, and have caught absolutely nothing at all."

Jesus just looks at Simon and smiles, in that special way he has, and that Simon would grow accustomed to and love so much.

"But at your word of instruction," mumbles Simon, "I will let down the net."

The fishermen draw the boat to the shore and Jesus steps out of the boat, onto the shingle beach. He stands on the pebbles and watches as the fishermen push off from the shore. The crowd pauses. They watch all this and a hush sweeps over them, as they watch Jesus' instruction being carried out. The fishermen are stripped to the waist and row out to deeper water. Peter and his brother Andrew let down the net. They are good at casting the net. They spread the net out just right. They watch it spread out and sink into the water until it is out of sight. The crowd watch them as well. Afterwards they are not sure whether they expect anything to be caught or not. Everything happens so quickly. It is the wrong time of day anyway. They are trying to please this special rabbi. To disobey would be to dishonour.

"Right!" says Peter. "Let's get it in."

"Here we go!" shouts back Andrew from the other end of the boat.

Together they begin to draw in the net. The net will be empty, and they will easily be able to pull it up and then they can go home. These thoughts fly through their minds. They are exhausted after the long night. They feel that the net is unusually heavy and hard to pull up. As it comes up to the surface, they can feel the movement and they know immediately what that is, as any fisherman will know. When the net comes to the surface it is not empty at all. It is full. Big, flapping fish splash the water of the sea everywhere churning up the surface of the water. There are loud gasps from the crowd who watch.

Peter and Andrew try to get the fish in. The net is too full and too heavy for just the two of them. They need help. They call to their partners in the other boat.

"James! John! Quickly!" they call out. "We need help!"

James and John, who are Simon's partners push out their boat as well to help with this amazing catch of fish. They begin to pull the net to shore as carefully as they can. It is so full of fish that it is close to breaking. They have had good catches before, but this catch of fish is bigger than any of them has ever seen before. They drag and row their way to the beach. It is a good thing that they were not too far out. Both boats are almost sinking. The catch of fish is so heavy. Both boats are full of big, flapping fish that shine bright in the bright sunlight.

Simon knows something for sure. This is no normal catch. It is a miracle. Tears came into his eyes as he looks at this teacher who stands on the shore and watches with a smile of approval on his face.

On the beach Simon falls at Jesus' knees. He feels weak and unworthy, at what Jesus has done.

"Please! You can't stay Lord. It is too much for me," says Simon, his eyes streaming with tears, overwhelmed by what Jesus has done.

"Don't be afraid," says Jesus, looking deep into Simon's eyes, "because from now on you will catch men, instead of fish."

When they had brought the fish onto the beach, they leave everything with their servants to finish up. They follow Jesus from that very moment. They become his disciples from that very day.

8.

Jesus Walks on Water

When people are desperate, they will do desperate things. They go out way beyond normal routines and comfort zones. Jesus is the light that has appeared for them. The one who can take them out of darkness. Out of the darkness of sickness, poverty and being ignored. Jesus is being followed by more and more desperate people. Never has there been anyone who has done the things that Jesus is doing. Jesus is not just doing good deeds. The things he does are plainly miracles. Who else can feed thousands of people with just a few loaves and a few fishes? Who else can heal the tragically outcast lepers? Who has ever given sight back to the blind, or made the deaf hear, the dumb talk and the lame walk? He is the one hope for the desperate.

Jesus cannot even go into the towns and villages any more. Now there is a growing group of people who want to make Jesus their king. They are even planning to do this by force. His disciples have just seen him feed thousands of people with just five loaves and two fish.

Jesus needs to be alone with his Father. They are on the shores of the Sea of Galilee, and the end of the day is fast approaching. The crowds are still with them and are quite content to be near this miracle worker. There is still some daylight time left. A gentle breeze blows, warm from across the waters Jesus sends his disciples on ahead of him.

"I want you to cross over again. Head for Bethsaida," says Jesus. "I will send the people away."

The disciples, tired now, prepare themselves and set off. They leave Jesus with the people and push off from the shore. It is a perfect evening.

Jesus blesses the people. He lays his hands on some of the children who come to him. He sends the last of the people away and chooses a place where he will pray. He walks up the steep side of a high hill close at hand. The slope rises from the sea and from this vantage point the lake is in clear view. Here he will not be disturbed. He needs to get away as he regularly does. He can pray here. The disciples know that as part of his routine Jesus will regularly be awake long before the sun rises. He will find a quiet place where he can pray. Often, he will spend the whole night praying.

Jesus knows what many of the people want of him. They want him to be their earthly king. He cannot let that happen. That is not his heavenly Father's will. He must move as one with his heavenly Father. He always speaks his Father's words and it is his Father who does the works.

Jesus looks out over the sea from the vantage point of the mountain. He can see his disciples in the boat way down in the middle of the sea. The wind is now against them and they are not able to use the sail. They are rowing. He can see that it is hard work for them. They are going but only very slowly.

The sun has now set. The moon is giving its light. The silver light of the moon shines on the dark waters of the sea. The light shimmers on the waves as the wind ruffles the water. The disciples in the middle of the sea don't feel quite the same when Jesus is not with them.

From where he is high up Jesus looks down on the sea below. He can see how the disciples are struggling along. He makes his way down to the sea picking his way carefully in the half-dark of the night. He keeps walking. At about three o'clock in the morning he comes to where the disciples are still struggling.

He is walking on the water. From the little fishing boat, and in the bright moonlight they can see a figure. Someone or something is walking across the water.

"A ghost!" someone shouts out.

What else can this be? It looks like the shape of a person. It can't be. That is impossible. It must be a ghost. There is more shouting as though that will scare off whatever this is. The rowing stops. The boat pitches and rolls as the disciples move in their fright. It seems like this figure is going to walk right past them. The figure seems to be on its way to the other side.

"Don't be afraid!" calls out Jesus. "It is I!"

"If it is you!" says Peter, "Tell me to come to you on the water!"

"Come!" comes the familiar sound of Jesus' voice, clear across the water.

Without another thought Peter swings his legs over the side of the boat. He begins somehow to walk towards Jesus. On the water. Peter can see the moonlight on Jesus as he gets closer. He is so focussed on this one that he loves so much. Still the word "Come" seems to vibrate in him. There is a fresh, strong gust of wind and the splash of a wave, that makes him look away, just for an instant. As he does he suddenly realizes the impossibility of what he is doing. At that he begins to sink. Jesus is now within arm's reach. Jesus reaches out strong arms and with that stops Peter from sinking down any further.

"Oh, little faith," says Jesus, and Peter can see in the moonlight the gentle face of the master and the deep love from his eyes. "Why did you doubt?"

The disciples recognize Jesus as he gets to the boat walking and supporting Peter. They recognize him as the moonlight shines on his face and clothes. They know him so well now. When they see him clearly their fear leaves them. Without any fuss they help him into the boat. He acts as though this is all quite normal as he in turn helps Peter in as well. The moon disappears and then reappears from behind a dark cloud and they know that it can only be Jesus.

This is the moment that everything changes. It is not something that happens gradually. It is immediate. As soon as he gets into the boat the strong wind that has been blowing stops. The disciples are stunned. They don't understand what is happening. They still have not quite understood what happened with the miracle of the loaves and fishes.

The rest of that journey feels dreamlike to the disciples although they know it is all too real. The moon shines its unearthly light. Jesus in the bow of the boat looks out to where they are heading.

When they land at Gennesaret the dawn is breaking and the local people are stirring, and the early risers are getting busy with their daily business. The people immediately recognize Jesus. They begin to spread the news that he is there. People begin to come to him from miles around. They carry sick people around on stretchers to wherever they hear Jesus is going to come next. They lay the sick people in the streets. The sick beg him that they might just touch his clothes as he walks past them. He allows them to do that. Everyone who touches him is immediately healed.

9.

The Ten Lepers

It may seem a strange thing to say but two thousand years ago, although it was very different in many ways, in other ways many things were just like today. There were diseases that the doctors could not cure just as there are today. Maybe the worst of these diseases was leprosy. It was a horrible disease and it is still around today in some places. Maybe one of the worst things about leprosy was that it was catchy.

They had special laws to try to stop this disease from spreading. As soon as anyone got the disease, they had to be separated from everyone else. They were not allowed to live with their families. They couldn't go into a town or a village. Others were terrified of also catching the disease.

This is the reason that anyone who got leprosy would have to live completely separated from everyone else. They were not allowed to have contact with other people. Lepers could only live with and be around other lepers. The families of lepers and other people who were kind would leave food out for them the way you would leave food out for a wild animal. They would leave food outside of the village or town so that when no-one was around the lepers could come and collect the food. In this way the lepers would at least have something to eat.

If a leper came too close to other people, the people would even throw stones at them, because they had been taught to be afraid of them. Lepers had to give a warning to others if they were walking along. If they met someone from a town on the road or in the countryside, they would have to call out their warning.

"Unclean! Unclean!" they would shout out.

There was a day when Jesus and his disciples are travelling along. It is a good road that the Romans have built, and it makes travelling from town to town so much easier. They are on their way to Jerusalem. On the way they must go through Samaria and Galilee. They talk as they go along.

They notice in the distance that there is a group of men standing some way off from the road. Their heads are covered so that you cannot really make out their faces. Their hands and feet are bandaged up.

125

These are ten people stand in the group and it seems as though all of them are men. When they see that it is Jesus passing by, they begin to shout out and they wave their arms to attract his attention. Like everyone else they know about Jesus and the miracles that he does. They are desperate and they shout, but now they are not shouting out, "Unclean! Unclean!" but rather they are shouting out for help.

"Master!" they call, "Jesus! Have mercy on us! Please help us!"

They are not embarrassed to shout out. Why would they be? What do they have to lose? This is their chance. They just happen to be there at the right time. If anyone can help them Jesus can. They need a miracle because that is the only way for them to be healed. They are lepers and they know that there is no doctor that can help them. What they need is nothing less than a miracle.

They have heard of so many that have been healed. If anyone needs Jesus, they know that they do and that makes them keep shouting from a distance. They get Jesus' attention and as he often has done and will often do again, he stops on the road. His disciples know that he will, and they stop as well. They have not known Jesus to turn anyone away who is in need.

He looks across at the men standing in that little group, who are not allowed to get closer and they grow quiet. The ten wait and there is a great expectancy that it will be today that something will happen to change everything for them. They wait to hear what Jesus will say? They have heard so many stories that the words of Jesus will change things and that when he speaks, he brings healing and miracles. As they wait expectantly, hope begins to stir in their hearts so that the distance to Jesus seems to be not so far. He feels very near to them.

"Go and show yourself to the priest!" calls out Jesus and his words carry clearly across the distance, to the ten men as they stand to the side of the road.

When they hear the words of Jesus something happens in their hearts that afterwards they will often talk about. They know that the only reason they should go and show themselves to the priest is when they are healed. They have dreamed of the moment when they can do this. They know the law well and that a leper who is healed must be examined by a priest to check that all signs of leprosy are gone. There are sacrifices that the priest must offer for the leper and then after seven days the priest must check that all the leprosy is gone, and he must sacrifice again on the eighth day. After that the leper will be declared to be healed. The priest will then give the one, now healed, permission to go back and live with their family and friends again.

They know what they must do and without hesitation these ten men set off. They don't stop to consider and there is no question whether they should do this or not. Immediately they start off because when a prophet speaks, they must simply obey. This command of Jesus will bring their healing.

What hope they know in that moment and such faith seems to fill their hearts. Their hopeless situation seems to be so small now as they walk towards Jerusalem. They keep off the road still, but they feel a difference in their bodies and that something is happening. The soreness in their joints begins to disappear. They look at each other as they go along, and they notice that the sores and marks on the skin of their faces begin to fade and disappear. They look closer at each other as they go along and what are frowns disappear and smiles come on to their faces. They laugh as clear skin appears even as they look at each other and they have not gone very far before their leprosy has completely disappeared.

They cannot contain their joy and their shuffle turns into a walk and then they begin to dance and laugh because they have no pain. They look at each other. They have got the miracle that they so need and want. They laugh with such relief at what is happening to them and began to now praise and thank God. They are no longer lepers and soon they will no longer be outcasts. They can live with their families again. They can lead a normal life. They will show themselves to the priest and he will do what the law needs to be done. It will only take seven days, and on the eighth day they will be free. The priest will make it public that they are healed.

The priest is amazed and takes the set time to make sure that they are quite healed. On the eighth day they are officially no longer lepers.

"You know what?" says one of the men who is healed. "I'm going to go back and thank Jesus for this."

"I want to get to go back home first," says another of the men. "I have so missed my family."

"Me too," the others agree, and they split up each one going on his own way home.

The man who turns back to thank Jesus is a Samaritan. The Jews and the Samaritans are not very good friends because they believe differently and have different ideas and different ways.

It is late when this man finds Jesus and the sun is beginning to set. He falls in front of Jesus and begins to thank him for this wonderful thing that Jesus has done for him. When the man has gone on his way home Jesus begins to speak to his followers.

"There were ten men who were healed," says Jesus. "What has happened to the other nine men? Did only one come back to give thanks to God. And that one is not even a Jew. Is it only a Samaritan who comes to thank God for his healing?"

Jesus

Do you want to become a follower of Christ? Read the prayer that I have included, and it will help you begin a wonderful and new life. Jesus has every answer for every situation.

Read also the other book, "Stories Jesus Told", and see the wisdom and understanding that he has and what the kingdom of God id like as well.

Jesus is one who loves people whether they are rich or poor, from every nation and language, and he loves you. He is able to forgive every wrong thing in our lives and to give us a brand-new start.

Read more about Jesus from the Bible, the one who came to earth from heaven to give us new life.

Prayer for Salvation

*9. That if thou shalt confess with thy mouth the Lord Jesus, and shalt believe in thine heart that God hath raised him from the dead, thou shalt be saved   10. For with the heart man believeth unto righteousness; and with the mouth confession is made unto salvation.
(Romans 10:9-10)*

Prayer

I believe that Jesus Christ died for my sins on the cross. I confess my sin and turn from it to Jesus .Come into my heart Lord Jesus.

I believe in my heart that God raised up Jesus from the dead so that I could have a new life and be born again. I therefore confess with my mouth that Jesus is my savior and I make Him Lord of my life. I am now a new creature. Old things have gone. All things in my life have become new.

(2 Corinthians 5 verse 17)

Contact Us

Website:
www.chrisbothaministries.com

e-mail address:
chrisbotha51@hotmail.com

Other Books by the Author

Principles of Christ

The Believers' Meeting

He is Alive

Miracles of Jesus

Children's Books are also available

All Books Available from

Amazon websites

Printed in Poland
by Amazon Fulfillment
Poland Sp. z o.o., Wrocław

58023379R00078